The Places You Can Go

Poems for Children

William Graham

© 2008

Text © William Graham 2008.

All rights reserved. No part of this book may be reproduced in any form or by any means, electronic or mechanical, including photocopying, recording or any information retrieval system, without prior permission in writing from the publishers.

ISBN-10: 1-4196-8378-0
EAN13: 978-1-4196-8378-7

Interior formatting/cover design by
Rend Graphics 2007
www.rendgraphics.com

Published by:
BookSurge Publishing
www.booksurge.com

To order additional copies, please visit:
www.amazon.com

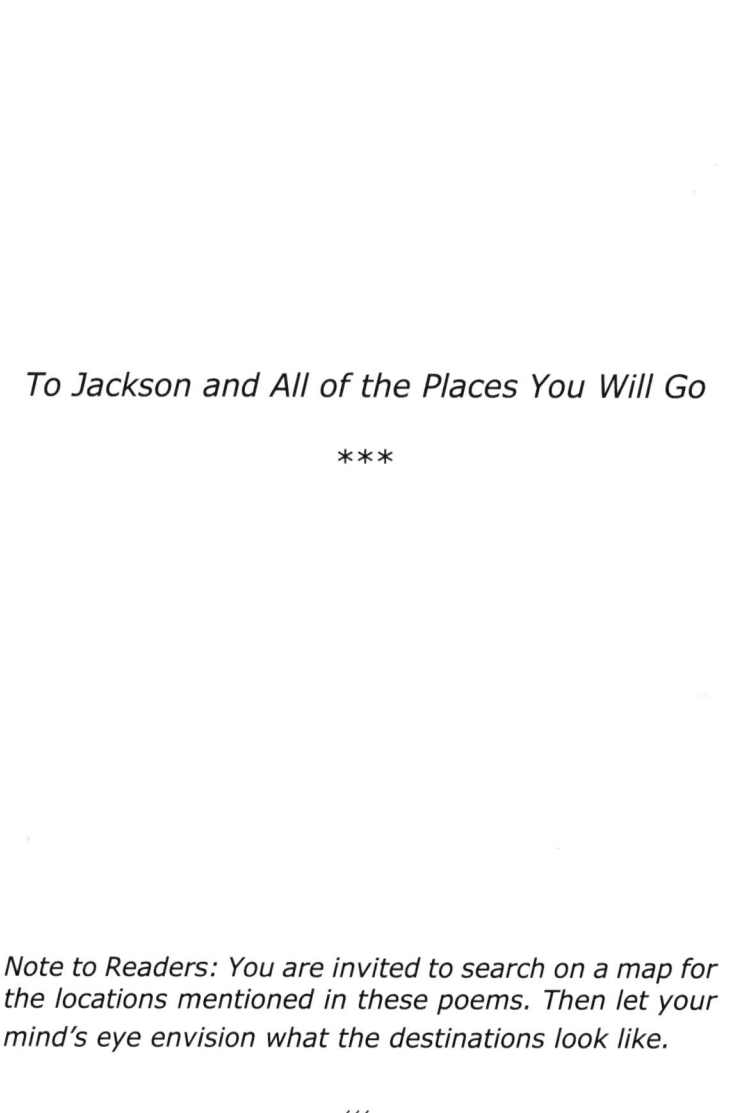

To Jackson and All of the Places You Will Go

***

Note to Readers: You are invited to search on a map for the locations mentioned in these poems. Then let your mind's eye envision what the destinations look like.

Arctic

The Places You Can Go

The Arctic

If you travel to the Arctic,
You will be on top of the world.
The wind is cold; the ice is thick.
Heavens around the North Star swirl.

Polar bears roam with fur of white.
They are smart, accomplished hunters.
Seals flee to the sea with a fright.
Staying would be a seal blunder.

If you travel to the Arctic,
Bring gloves and a warm down jacket;
For the frigid air hits you quick.
As for a hat? Make sure you pack it!

Arctic

The North Pole

The great white north
Has inspired many adventurers
From their earliest years on earth.
They are willing to endure temperatures

Of sixty below zero to trek across
The frozen Arctic sea
With faces caked in frost
Just for a place in history.

Many died on their way to the pole;
Forever lost in the shifting ice.
Their loved ones were consoled;
Husbands and fathers had been sacrificed.

The pull of the North Pole remains strong
For those whose spirit seeks to wander.
Maybe one day you will take your place among
The trekkers drawn by the pole's allure.

The Places You Can Go

Iceland

The Vikings arrived hundreds of years back.
They came from Norway in ships long and strong.
They were conquerors, ready to attack.
But the isle was empty. They rowed headlong

Onto the black sand shore and found green fields
To rear children, cattle and sheep.
Each year, the island more beauty revealed.
Nature made even warriors weep.

To keep intruders away from their land
They put "Ice" in the name of their home.
"Let people think this is a cold wasteland;
This is our jewel. No more will we roam."

Antarctica

The Places You Can Go

Antarctica

You won't fall off the earth in Antarctica
In spite of what some people may say.
Even though you are at the bottom of the world,
There's this useful thing called gravity.

For what's down can be up;
It's all from your point of view.
So travel as far south as you can go—
To where all the stars above will be new.

Antarctica

The Penguin Ball

They have no need for designer clothes.
They come as they are in their black and white.
Many have taken an afternoon doze
To prepare to party through the night.

They come in all sizes—some short and some tall.
They come from long distances on the glacial plateau.
When invitations go out for the penguin ball,
No one declines—everyone must show.

They step lightly across the ice
In elegant groups of two or three.
When the ball begins, everyone is nice;
Past hurts are forgotten—no one is an enemy.

The ball is the highlight of the Antarctic night.
The penguins need an event to let off some steam
When biting winds howl and darkness grips tight.
It's the time for penguins to relax in the extreme.

The Places You Can Go

The Land of Extremes

If you want to go the highest,
Driest, coldest place on earth—
To Antarctica you must go.

Tell you parents and friends
That it must be so—
To Antarctica you must go.

A white sand beach beneath
Skies blazing with a tropical glow? No—
To Antarctica you must go.

You were born to explore
Places others do not wish to know—
To Antarctica you must go!

North America

North America

The Places You Can Go

A Secret Place

A secret place my friends and I did share.
We told nobody the why or the where.
It was up a hill and down a valley.
It was hidden under a tall oak tree.
There we laughed and played until the sun set.
I have grown, but I will never forget
The safe, secret place where there was no chores;
Just a time to be friends in the outdoors.

North America

Monster in the Room

I hear a loud sound. Is it in my head?
Or is there a monster under my bed?
I crawl under the warm covers to hide.
The noise goes away. I peek out and spy
A large black shadow dancing in my room.
It is no monster, as I had assumed.
It is instead a shadow of a tree
That is banging on my window. I see
Now that it is a clear, cold windy night.
No monsters—just a tree in the moonlight.

The Places You Can Go

Maine Mooses

In the dense forests of Maine,
There live houses with antlers called mooses.
The male is gigantic; he goes where he chooses.
"This is my domain," he does proclaim.

The female is smaller, but still imposing.
Confident and proud, she makes no excuses.
But she and her friends are shy forest recluses.
They prefer mooses only when convening.

If you are hiking on a path in Maine,
Keep watch for the tanks with legs called mooses.
They like privacy; to their families they will not introduce us.
So just move along and forgive their disdain.

North America

The Seasons in Maine

Along the rocky coast of Maine,
Fog walks in like an unwanted guest;
And not far behind it is the autumn rain,
Signaling that summer will take a rest.

Pine trees are shrouded by low clouds and mist.
Maple leaves crunch and crackle on the ground.
Snow and cold are coming, winter insists.
The north wind's whistle is the only sound.

Winter has locked the door and hidden the key.
The rocks along the ocean are caked in ice.
The forest dreams of a spring reverie.
But for now patience must suffice.

The Places You Can Go

The Green Mountains

When you go hiking with your parents
In the mountains they call green,
As you reach the rocky summit
You will find a glorious scene.

For spread out below you
As far as the eye can see,
Are mountains kissing the sky
As they cradle many a secluded valley.

Even in summer, the air will be chilled.
And you may be whipped by wind from the north.
But just sit there and drink in the sights
Until to the next mountain you go forth.

North America

Maple Syrup

In Vermont's deep forests
Old men screw taps into maple trees;
By drip, drip, drip relentless
Sap flows into buckets slow as you please.

The sap is turned into thick syrup,
To be poured over pancakes galore.
Remember next time as a bottle you pick up—
The sweet liquid comes from a tree—not a store.

The Places You Can Go

The White Mountains

When the calendar turns to October,
The White Mountains are not white.
Explosions of red and gold are seen there.
Thousands flock to see this glorious sight.

Scientists are not sure why the leaves
Change each year from green to red.
"It's like a sunscreen," one person believes.
"It's to keep bugs away," another has said.

Whatever the reason, one thing is sure:
The White Mountains of New Hampshire
For a time wear many colors that do not endure.
Soon winter returns with its all-white attire.

North America

Country Dark

In the country, you will find the darkest dark.
Take a flashlight before you embark,
Or everything you encounter will be a question mark.

On foggy nights when there is no moon,
You will feel like you're inside a black balloon.
You will stumble and fall like a buffoon.

But there are nights when the sky explodes with stars,
Sending sparks at the speed of light from here to Mars.
On such nights we are thankful that this country home is ours.

The Places You Can Go

Lake Champlain's Monster

In the cold depths of Lake Champlain
Lurks a creature no one can explain.
Sailors have told of a coal-black serpent;
Their ships this long shadow does torment.

Ships have been burned by the monster's fire.
Sailors swear this is true—do not call them liars.
Ships have been crushed by its thorny black tail
That whirls like a tornado and is larger than a whale.

When you go sailing on the waters of Lake Champlain,
Beware as you enter the serpent's domain.
He is watching you with his iron eyes;
He is waiting to catch you by surprise.

North America

The Legacy of Ice

The state of Montana
Was once covered in thick ice
Called glaciers—not a
Plant or animal escaped demise.

For centuries, the ice ruled the land,
But block by icy block it began to retreat,
Scooping out lakes and valleys with a cold hand.
Flowers bloomed; on high peaks eagles took a seat.

Today the land is a large park,
Stunning in its glacial legacy.
People young and old go there to embark
On hikes of grand views and serenity.

South America

The Places You Can Go

Above the Andes

The jagged Andes mountains slice the Peruvian sky;
Their snow-covered peaks glowing in the dawn.
A graceful condor swirls above a remote valley;
Relying on speed and cunning rather than brawn.

With brown wings more than ten-feet wide,
The condor soars majestically on Andean breezes.
Circling and circling, then hanging in a glide.
Content to move as the wind pleases.

South America

Cuzco Nights

The air chills fast as the sun drops on Cuzco,
The sturdy ancient capital of the Incas.
The natives wrap themselves in llama wool as they go
Home from their shops. Some pause

To listen to a man playing a flute in the square.
The thick stone walls of the city have survived
Wars and earthquakes, but are still standing there—
A solid legacy of Inca grace and pride.

A full moon rises from behind the peaks,
Showering Cuzco in silken yellow light.
People climb steep paths to return home and speak
Of another day passed at twelve-thousand feet of height.

The Places You Can Go

Patagonia

There is no place like Patagonia,
Nestled at the bottom of Argentina.
It is nature's unique symphonia,
Composed to dazzle and awe.

Gauchos ride the plains
Enduring heat and rains,
While viewing dazzling terrain.
It is nature unrestrained.

South America

Llamas

On steep mountain paths in Peru
You may see a sight new to you;
And you may be a little confused.

You will see loads of llamas
Sitting in their best pajamas
Partaking in an Andean nirvana.

They get bored with their wool coats it seems;
They like to dazzle like models in magazines,
Showing off bright reds and glowing greens.

They prance and preen and try to impress;
Some mama llamas talk of looking for a dress.
If only this year's fashions they could possess.

The Places You Can Go

Machu Picchu

High in the steamy jungle,
Hidden from intruders' sight,
Perches an ancient city
Of wonder and delight.

It's called Machu Picchu
By the natives of the land—
Home to the high priests
And those at their command.

Spanish invaders could not find it,
Although they mightily tried.
They bribed and threatened;
But to them the people would not confide.

For centuries the jungle slowly embraced
Machu Picchu's homes and fields;
But it has been rediscovered and restored;
Its mysterious glory once again unconcealed.

South America

Amazonia

If you want to travel a river long,
Look no farther than the Amazon.

Sticky jungle heat
Is what you will meet

As you float from Peru
To the Atlantic blue.

Monkeys chatter in the trees,
Then leap from limb to limb with ease.

Snakes and crocodiles lurk
In the water warm and dark.

Do you have the spirit to go there—
Into the deepest, darkest Amazonia?

Europe

The Places You Can Go

Paris, France

In Paris, people do not say "Hello."
You must learn to say "Bonjour" if you go.
After you have had a pastry or two,
To feel at home, here is what you should do:
Say "Au revoir" as you bid them adieu.
It's time to stroll along the river Seine.
Enjoy the view; you might not return again.
You glance at your watch and note the late hour.
You must rush; time to see the Eiffel Tower!

Europe

Paris Sewers

Paris is renowned for its parks and museums,
But I just get bored when I see them.
Give me a place that's not so debonair,
Let me tell you about the Paris sewers!
You descend underground to the dark and damp;
Watch your step as you carry your lamp.
Soon you reach a huge stone tunnel,
You listen as your guide Marcel
Tells you how the sewers snake
Under homes and offices to take
Away the things that we flush.
You know what I mean. Why blush?
As you walk along looking at this and that,
Pay attention—you may see a Parisian rat!
I know that sewers are not for everyone,
But even in sewers, Paris will not be outdone!

The Places You Can Go

Scottish Highlands

Deep in the Scottish Highlands,
Above a crystal blue lake,
A boy named Ian
Decides which path to take.

He chooses a trail through a meadow;
There runs a trout-filled brook.
His father once fished there,
Showing Ian how to bait a hook.

Now Ian is old enough
To trek through the Highlands alone.
On days sunny or blustery,
The craggy peaks he calls his own.

Europe

Ireland

From north to south and all places in between,
The color of Ireland is a deep emerald green.

The fields are full of sheep filling themselves with grass;
Mountains rise from blue lakes as still as plates of glass.

The Irish are fond of telling tall tales of old—
About leprechauns who protect pots of gold.

No "little people" really live at the rainbow's end;
But sometimes it's nice to laugh and pretend.

For the Irish love a joke and a smile;
That's why Ireland always beguiles.

The Places You Can Go

Norway

Mountains touch the sea in places called fjords.
Can't pronounce the word? It rhymes with "swords."

Norway is home to herds of reindeer,
Whose antlers tower above their ears.

They prance through the ice and snow,
In temperatures of sixty below.

Reindeer survive quite nicely in the arctic night;
Twenty-four hours of darkness does not give them a fright.

But they too like summer's light and feeling warm;
When flowers bloom and honey bees swarm.

Reindeer families relax in the northern sun,
After winter's chill, it's time for some Norwegian fun.

Europe

The Alps

From Mont Blanc's summit, stand
And peer into three countries.
You can swoosh to Switzerland,
Italy and France on your skis.

If you get tired on your way,
Take a break for some hot chocolate
At a sunny Swiss Alpine chalet.
Then ski back to France for dinner at eight.

Tomorrow after you have had a long sleep,
Return to the peak for more Alpine fun.
Head to Italy on a trail long and steep,
Stop for spaghetti before you are done.

The Places You Can Go

Rome

The ancient Romans loved to build
On a colossal scale.
Thousands of workers hauled marble
And stone over hill and dale.

Rome's glory days have now passed away,
But grand monuments remain.
The Coliseum and Pantheon
Recall past emperors' reigns.

When you walk on old Roman roads,
Close you eyes and imagine
The chariots of Julius Caesar
Heading off to battle barbarians.

Africa

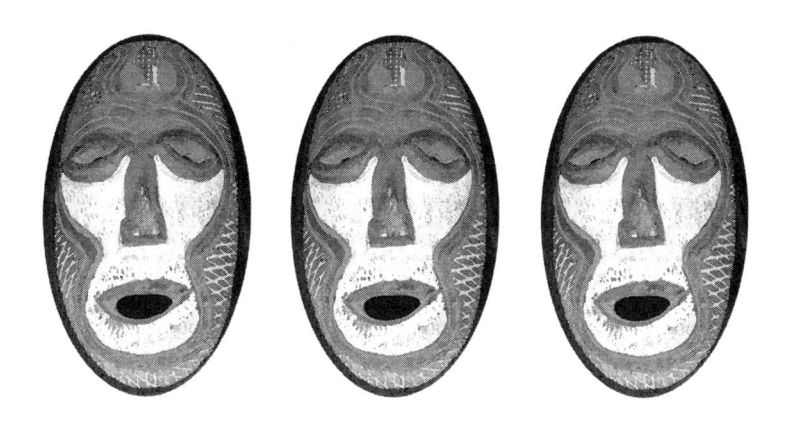

The Places You Can Go

Pyramids

In Egypt, to the west of Cairo,
Loom the tombs of the pharaohs.

Their triangular bulk rises from the sand,
One of the seven wonders created by man.

Scavengers have destroyed much of their glory.
The Sahara desert sands hide the rest of the story.

Africa

Safari

The merciless African sun parches the vast plains,
Where lions lurk in the bush for their prey.
Zebras and gazelles stand still and are wary
Of any sound or motion in the vast terrain.

In the distance, a herd of elephants plods along,
Using their great memory to find a watering hole,
They bellow with glee as in the mud they roll;
Mothers sing their babies asleep with elephant songs.

As the sun closes the door on your African day,
You sit besides a campfire next to a tent.
Then from the darkness great roars are sent;
You wonder if the lions are having a zebra buffet!

The Places You Can Go

The Mighty Nile

When the moon shines on the Nile,
It sparkles like a diamond
As it flows for mile after mile
Between dunes of sand.

When the sun hovers over the Nile
Like a fireball in the sky,
Scores of hungry crocodiles
Wait patiently, showing just their cruel eyes.

Night and day the Nile flows
From the jungle to the sea,
Sometimes fast, sometimes slow,
But always with African majesty.

Africa

Kilimanjaro's Shadow

Kilimanjaro is the highest spot in Africa;
It towers above the plains below.
In a world of heat and dust,
The mountain's peak has a cap of snow.

A leopard's body was once found near the top;
Many people thought this could not be true.
A leopard would not find food so high;
But maybe the cat climbed just to enjoy the view.

It's a mystery that may not be solved.
Not all of Africa's secrets may we know.
But we should not abandon the search;
Answers may yet be found in Kilimanjaro's shadow.

Asia

The Places You Can Go

The Great Wall

The Great Wall slithers like a snake
Over mountains and down deep valleys in China.
Armies of tourists converge to take
Photos of themselves amidst the hoopla.

Built to keep marauding invaders out,
The wall has crumbled in many places.
Only foolish emperors could have thought
That nature and warriors would not deface it.

Asia

Top of the World

In the country of Nepal, north of India,
You can touch the sky in the Himalayas.
The highest mountains in the world are there—
Peaks of snow, cold and thin air.

Among all of these mountains, one is the greatest—
It's the summit known as Mount Everest.
There is no spot higher on the planet.
Mountaineers dream of standing on it.

The Places You Can Go

Tiger, Tiger

In the Asian jungles, tigers prowl,
Sniffing for prey in the twilight.
They move silently, with not even a growl,
As they stalk and prepare to bite.

They rule their jungle domains
With a regal feline snarl.
All other creatures know the tiger remains
A neighbor with whom they must not quarrel.

Australia

The Places You Can Go

Kangaroos

The lighting bolt of brown that you see
Leaping across the outback
Is an Australian kangaroo—
Leaving in the dust its gigantic tracks.

With feet like canoe paddles,
Kangaroos are Olympic leapers.
No fence or ditch is their match.
Their tails are like giant sweepers.

Mother kangaroos carry their babies
In soft warm belly pouches.
After such pampering, it's no wonder
That kangaroos are sweet—not grouches.

Australia

Down Under

Australia is known as the land Down Under.
But the rain still falls down, not up;
Winds still swirl and the earth shakes with thunder.

Koalas, wallabies and platypuses
Are just some of the weird and rare creatures
Who inhabit Australia's trees and bushes.

From rain forests in the north
To vast deserts in the center,
Australia is the largest island on earth.

The Places You Can Go

Great Barrier Reef

The jellyfish said to the grouper:
"Welcome to the Great Barrier Reef."
The grouper exclaimed: "This place is super!"

"It's full of colorful coral that's pleasing to the eye,
Warm blue water that keeps me toasty,
And juicy morsels to eat in great supply."

"It's a grand place," replied the jellyfish.
"It's all about location, location, location.
But be careful or you may end up as somebody's dish."

"I will heed your warning, kind sir" the grouper said.
"I don't want to be my neighbor's entrée;
I much prefer to do the eating instead!"

Oceania

The Places You Can Go

Stone Heads of Easter Island

Far in the South Pacific,
There is a small volcanic island
Where giant stone heads stick
Out of the wind-swept lava wasteland.

The people of Easter Island
Carved these massive monuments
For the families royal—whose command
The islanders never passed judgment.

Hour after aching hour, day after day,
Workers carved by hand under tropical
Heat and rain—their skill displayed
To both their allies and rivals.

The natives of Easter Island
Have long since gone to their graves;
But looming over the black sand
Are frozen faces, never seeing or hearing the waves.

Oceania

Hawaii

For the people of Hawaii,
"Aloha" means both hello and goodbye.
It's a word that's fun to say
As your tan yourself under the Pacific sky.

Some tourists go there to surf;
Others stay dry on the lush turf.
Some climb volcanoes for a grand view.
Some dive deep into the warm ocean blue.

From Lanai to Kauai,
From Oahu to Maui,
The garden isles of Hawaii
Have been a paradise for centuries.

The Places You Can Go

New Zealand

East of Australia,
North of Antarctica,
Lie the islands of New Zealand—
A natural wonderland.

A long way from anywhere,
You lose a day just getting there.
But greeting you will be
Mountains that plunge to the sea.

Rain forests and glaciers abound;
Birds called Kiwis can also be found.
Hike, sail or ski—you can do it all
If New Zealand is your port of call.

Oceania

Polynesia

Small islands glimmer in the Pacific like pearls,
Stretching for thousands of miles across the sea.
They are part of Polynesia—
One is called Fiji, another Tahiti.

But there are thousands of islands with no name,
Just small specks of coral in the blue infinity,
Where palm trees sway in the trade winds,
And from horizon to horizon there is nothing to see.

For centuries islanders sailed from place to place,
Navigating by the winds and constellations,
They searched for new lands to live and farm;
Now people go to these islands for tropical vacations.

Made in the USA